DECLUTTERING FOR SENIORS: A SENIOR'S GUIDE TO DECLUTTERING YOUR LITERARY LEGACY

Your Guide for Decluttering Your Mind and Body

DR AMELIA BRIDGES

Why This Book is Different

Have you ever looked at your overflowing bookshelves and felt both love and overwhelm? You're not alone. As we age, our book collections often grow into more than just reading material – they become part of who we are. But there comes a time when managing these collections becomes challenging. Maybe you've noticed it's harder to dust around countless books, or perhaps you're planning to downsize your home. Whatever your reason, this book understands that decluttering books isn't just about clearing space – it's about honoring your life's reading journey while making your living space more comfortable and safe.

Unlike general decluttering guides, this book focuses specifically on the unique challenges seniors face with their book collections. We won't just tell you to "get rid of books you don't need." Instead, we'll walk through practical solutions that respect your emotional attachments while helping you create a more manageable and enjoyable living space. Whether you're dealing with hundreds of books or thousands, this guide will help you make thoughtful decisions about your literary collection.

Chapter 1: Your Books, Your Story

Every book on your shelf tells two stories: the one written on its pages and the one about why it matters to you. That worn copy of "To Kill a Mockingbird" might be the one you taught from during your teaching career. The collection of mystery novels might remind you of cozy evenings spent reading with your late spouse. Understanding why we keep books is the first step in making mindful decisions about them.

In this chapter, we'll explore why letting go of books can feel particularly challenging for our generation. Many of us grew up when books were precious possessions, passed down through families or saved up for with care. We'll look at how these deep connections influence our decisions today and learn to distinguish between books that still serve a purpose in our lives and those that might better serve others.

Take Martha, age 75, who kept every book her children had ever read. When she finally sorted through them, she realized she could keep one or two special titles from each child's collection and photograph the rest. Now these precious memories take up less space, but the stories and emotions remain just as strong.

Chapter 2: Health and Safety First

Did you know that a single shelf of books can collect up to a cup of dust per year? Or that reaching for heavy books on high shelves is one of the leading causes of falls among seniors? In this chapter, we'll talk about why organizing your books isn't just about tidiness – it's about your health and safety.

We'll explore practical ways to arrange your books so they don't become hazards. For instance, Bob, age 82, moved all his frequently-read books to shelves at waist height after his doctor warned him about the risks of reaching overhead. This simple change made his daily reading more enjoyable and much safer.

You'll learn how to identify when books might be affecting your air quality and what to do about it. We'll also discuss simple solutions like using bookends to prevent avalanches and arranging books so they're easy to access without straining.

Chapter 3: The Digital Revolution

Remember when we thought nothing could replace the feel of a real book? While that's still true in many ways, digital books have opened up exciting new possibilities for seniors. Imagine being able to make any book's text larger with just a tap, or reading at night without straining your eyes thanks to built-in lighting.

In this chapter, we'll explore how e-readers can help you keep your entire library in a device lighter than a paperback. We'll look at how Sarah, age 70, managed her arthritis better after switching to an e-reader – no more struggling to hold heavy hardcovers open. You'll learn which digital devices might work best for you and how to access thousands of free books through your local library's digital collection.

Don't worry if technology makes you nervous – we'll break everything down into simple steps and explain exactly how these tools can make reading easier and more enjoyable as we age.

Chapter 4: The Five-Step Sorting System

Facing a lifetime of books can feel overwhelming. That's why we've developed a simple but effective way to sort your books into five clear categories. This isn't about making quick decisions – it's about thinking through each book's role in your life today and tomorrow.

We'll walk through real examples, like Helen's experience sorting through fifty years of cookbooks. She kept the ones with her hand-written notes and family recipes (Keep and Display), photographed her favorite recipes from others (Digitize), gave special ones to her grandchildren (Pass to Family), and donated the rest to a culinary school (Donate).

This chapter provides clear criteria for each category, helping you make decisions you'll feel good about both now and later.

Chapter 5: Creating Your Literary Legacy

Books carry our memories, and passing them on thoughtfully can be one of life's most meaningful gifts. This chapter isn't just about deciding which books to give away – it's about sharing the stories behind them.

We'll explore how to create a meaningful collection for future generations. Like Frank, who created a special bookshelf of signed first editions for his grandchildren, complete with notes about how he acquired each book and why it mattered to him. You'll learn how to document your reading history and create personal inscriptions that transform ordinary books into family treasures.

Chapter 6: Practical Solutions for Storage

Good storage isn't just about having enough shelves – it's about creating a system that works for you today. In this chapter, we'll look at practical ways to organize books so they're easy to access and enjoy. You'll learn how Tom, age 78, reorganized his history collection by creating a comfortable reading nook with good lighting and his favorite books within easy reach.

We'll discuss different storage solutions that take into account common challenges like arthritis or limited mobility. From adjustable shelving to book covers that prevent dust, you'll discover ways to make your book collection work better for your current lifestyle.

Chapter 7: The Joy of Sharing

There's something special about passing a beloved book into the right hands. This chapter explores the many rewarding ways to share your books with others who will appreciate them. Whether it's helping stock a school library, contributing to a senior center's collection, or sharing with family members, you'll discover how letting go can create new connections.

We'll share stories like Margaret's, who donated her collection of art books to a local community college and now enjoys visiting "her" books in their new home. You'll learn about different ways to donate books and how to ensure they find the best possible new homes.

Chapter 8: Maintaining Your Curated Collection

Once you've decluttered your books, keeping your collection manageable becomes much easier with the right system. This chapter shows you how to maintain your newly organized library without feeling overwhelmed.

You'll learn practical tips like the one-in-one-out rule that helped James keep his mystery collection from overtaking his apartment. We'll discuss simple cleaning routines that protect both your books and your health, and how to rotate books seasonally to keep your collection fresh and interesting.

Chapter 9: Digital Resources and Community

Today's technology offers amazing ways to enjoy books while taking up less physical space. This chapter introduces you to digital resources that can enhance your reading life, from library apps that deliver books to your tablet to online communities where you can discuss your favorite reads.

We'll explore how Mary, age 68, discovered audiobooks during her daily walks, and how Bill uses his library's online system to access large-print books from home. You'll learn about reliable digital resources and simple ways to connect with other readers online.

Chapter 10: Living Lighter, Reading Better

The final chapter celebrates your journey to a more manageable book collection. We'll look at how other seniors have found freedom in having fewer, but more meaningful books. Like Diana, who says she enjoys reading more now that she can easily find and access the books she loves.

We'll discuss how to handle new book acquisitions mindfully and how to continue adapting your collection as your needs change. Most importantly, we'll explore how having fewer books can actually enrich your reading life and create space for new experiences.

Conclusion: Your New Chapter

As we wrap up our journey together, remember that decluttering your books isn't about giving up your love of reading – it's about creating a more enjoyable and manageable way to live with books. Whether you've decided to keep 50 books or 500, what matters is that your collection now brings you joy without causing stress or safety concerns.

This conclusion offers encouragement for maintaining your progress and embracing the freedom that comes with a well-curated book collection. You'll find reminders of key strategies and inspiration for continuing your journey toward a more organized and enjoyable reading life.

Your Books, Your Story

When Margaret turned eighty, her children suggested she might want to "do something" about her books. They meant well, but their words made her heart sink. The books filling her living room shelves, stacked on her bedside table, and lining her hallway weren't just objects taking up space – they were memories, achievements, and dreams. Each one told a story beyond the words printed on its pages.

If you're like Margaret, you understand that feeling. Our books become part of who we are, especially after decades of collecting them. This chapter will help you understand why your book collection means so much to you and how to make thoughtful decisions about its future.

Why We Collect Books

Think back to your first special book. Maybe it was a gift from a parent, a prize at school, or a treasure you saved up to buy yourself. For many of us who grew up in the 1940s, 50s, or 60s, books were precious possessions. They weren't just entertainment – they were gateways to knowledge and adventure at a time when information wasn't available at the touch of a screen.

Tom, age 78, remembers saving his paper route money for three months to buy a complete set of encyclopedias. "Those books represented everything I wanted to learn about the world," he says. "Even now, sixty years later, I can't look at an encyclopedia without remembering that feeling of possibility."

We collect books for many reasons:

Knowledge and Learning: Many of us grew up believing that books were the key to a better life through education. That's why your shelves might be filled with textbooks from college courses, professional development books from your career, or self-help guides that marked important life transitions.

Emotional Connections: Books often represent relationships and memories. That cookbook might be precious because it contains your mother's handwritten notes. The worn copy of "Goodnight Moon" reminds you of reading to your children and grandchildren.

Status and Achievement: For our generation, having a full bookshelf often represented success and cultivation. Being well-read was a mark of accomplishment, and our book collections showed that we valued learning and culture.

Security and Comfort: Growing up in times of uncertainty, books represented stability. They were something solid you could count on, offering comfort and escape when needed.

The Special Challenge for Seniors

Letting go of books is challenging at any age, but it's particularly difficult for seniors. Here's why:

Generational Values: We grew up in an era when books were expensive and treated with respect. The idea of getting rid of a perfectly good book might feel wasteful or wrong. Jean, age 72, shares, "My parents taught me never to throw away books. It feels almost disrespectful to consider it now."

Life Review: As we age, we naturally spend more time reflecting on our lives. Books can be powerful triggers for memories, making them seem even more precious. That history book isn't just about World War II – it's about the conversations you had with your father about his service.

Loss of Control: Many seniors feel they're constantly being asked to give things up – driving, certain activities, maybe even their home. In this context, being asked to part with books can feel like yet another loss of control over their lives.

Physical Limitations: The practical task of sorting through books can be physically challenging. This can make the project feel overwhelming before it even begins.

Understanding Your Book Relationship

Before you make any decisions about your books, it's important to understand your personal relationship with them. Take a moment to answer these questions (you might want to write down your answers):

1. When you look at your books, what feelings come up first?
2. Which books do you actually read or reference regularly?
3. Which books represent important memories or relationships?
4. Which books do you keep out of habit or obligation?

Sarah, age 75, did this exercise and discovered something interesting. "I realized I was keeping all my old nursing textbooks because they represented my career identity," she says. "But I hadn't opened them in twenty years, and medical knowledge has changed so much they're not even accurate anymore. Understanding this helped me let them go."

Different Types of Book Attachments

As we explore your book collection, it's helpful to recognize different types of attachments:

Active Attachments: These are books you currently use and enjoy. Maybe you reread your favorite mystery novels every few years, or regularly consult your gardening guides. These books are still serving an active purpose in your life.

Memory Attachments: These books are valuable for the memories they hold, not their content. Your child's first reader, a book signed by a beloved author, or a novel that got you through a difficult time might fall into this category.

Identity Attachments: These books represent who you are or were – the college professor's academic books, the artist's collection of art books, the traveler's travel guides. They're part of how you see yourself.

Aspirational Attachments: These are books you always meant to read or skills you hoped to learn. They represent dreams and intentions rather than current realities.

Future-Use Attachments: Books you're keeping because you think you (or someone else) might need them someday.

Practical Needs Versus Emotional Attachments

Now comes the challenging part – distinguishing between emotional attachments and practical needs. Here's a simple way to evaluate each book:

Practical Questions:

• Have you read or referenced this book in the past year?

• Is the information still current and accurate?

• Can you easily access and handle this book?

• Do you have space to store it properly?

Emotional Questions:

• Does this book bring back important memories?

• Would you feel a sense of loss without it?

• Does it represent an important part of your identity?

• Are you keeping it out of guilt or obligation?

Consider Barbara's experience. At 83, she had hundreds of books on European history, her lifetime passion. When evaluating her collection, she realized she could divide it into three categories:

1. Books she still regularly referenced (about 20%)

2. Books with her personal notes and marginalia that represented her scholarly work (about 10%)

3. Books she hadn't opened in years and could easily find at the library if needed (about 70%)

This clarity helped her make decisions about what to keep and what to let go.

Making Peace with Change

One of the most important things to understand is that letting go of books doesn't mean letting go of memories or knowledge. Frank, age 79, found a creative solution: "I photographed the covers and title pages of books that had special meaning but that I knew I wouldn't read again. I created a digital album with notes about why each book was important to me. Now my grandchildren can understand my life through books without inheriting boxes of them."

Remember:

• Your identity isn't dependent on owning certain books

• Memories remain even when physical objects are gone

• Making space for what serves you now honors both your past and present

• Passing books along allows them to touch new lives

Practical Steps Forward

As you begin thinking about your book collection, try these steps:

1. Start Small: Choose one shelf or category of books to evaluate first. This makes the process less overwhelming.

2. Sort into Clear Categories:

∘ Keep and Use: Books you actively read or reference

∘ Keep for Memory: Important books with strong emotional attachments

∘ Consider Letting Go: Books you haven't touched in years

∘ Definitely Let Go: Outdated or damaged books

3. Ask Key Questions:

∘ Would I choose to buy this book today?

∘ Does keeping this book make my life better?

∘ Could someone else benefit more from this book now?

4. Take Your Time: There's no rush to make decisions. You can sort through books gradually, giving each the consideration it deserves.

Looking Forward

As you work through understanding your relationship with your books, remember that the goal isn't to get rid of books – it's to create a collection that serves and brings you joy in your current life. Some people might keep hundreds of books, others just a few dozen. What matters is that your decision feels right for you.

Eleanor, age 85, sums it up well: "After I understood why I was keeping each book, making decisions became easier. I kept the books that still make me happy, found good homes for the others, and now I actually read more because I can find the books I want without getting overwhelmed."

Chapter Summary

• Book collections hold deep meaning for seniors due to generational values and life experiences

• Understanding different types of book attachments helps in making decisions

• Distinguishing between emotional attachments and practical needs is key

• There's no single "right" way to manage your collection

• Taking time to make thoughtful decisions leads to better outcomes

• Letting go of books doesn't mean letting go of memories

Reflection Questions

Before moving on to the next chapter, consider:

1. What are the three most important books in your collection and why?

2. Which books do you keep out of obligation rather than desire?

3. What would your ideal book collection look like?

4. How do you want your books to serve you in this phase of your life?

Remember, understanding your relationship with your books is the first step toward creating a collection that brings you joy without causing stress or overwhelm. In the next chapter, we'll look at practical ways to make your book collection safer and more accessible.

Health and Safety First

When Ruth slipped while reaching for a book on her top shelf, she was lucky her daughter was visiting and could help her up. "I never thought my books could be dangerous," she said later. "I've been reaching for books on that shelf for thirty years." But as we age, even familiar activities can become risky. This chapter will help you understand how to make your book collection safer and more manageable.

The Hidden Challenges of Book Collections

Books bring us joy, but they can also create unexpected problems as we age. Here's what you need to know about keeping yourself safe while enjoying your library.

Weight Matters

A single hardcover book might weigh between one and five pounds. That doesn't sound like much until you're lifting a stack of them or reaching overhead to grab one. Consider these facts:

• A shelf of hardcover books can weigh 30-40 pounds

• Medical guidelines suggest seniors should avoid lifting more than 10-15 pounds without assistance

• Reaching overhead with even small weights increases fall risk significantly

Dorothy, age 77, learned this the hard way: "I was moving some books to dust behind them and didn't realize how heavy they were together. I strained my back and couldn't garden for weeks."

Space and Movement

Books have a way of creeping into our walking paths. What starts as a neat stack can become a hazard:

• Books on the floor can be trip hazards

• Piles of books can make it harder to use walking aids like canes or walkers

• Crowded spaces make it difficult to maintain balance

• Emergency exits might become blocked

Robert, age 82, made an important observation: "I used to keep books on my bedside table, but when I started using a walker, I realized I needed that space clear for safety."

The Invisible Problem: Dust and Air Quality

Books are dust magnets, and this creates more than just a housekeeping challenge. Here's what happens when books collect dust:

Health Impact

• Dust mites thrive in book collections, especially in warm, humid conditions

• Old books can harbor mold spores

• Paper deterioration releases particles into the air

• Dust accumulation can trigger:

◦ Allergies

◦ Asthma

◦ Respiratory irritation

◦ Sinus problems

Mary, age 73, shares her experience: "I couldn't figure out why my allergies were worse in my study until my doctor asked about my books. Once I removed some books and started regular cleaning, my breathing improved dramatically."

Practical Solutions for Dust Control

1. Regular Cleaning Schedule:

◦ Dust books weekly using a microfiber cloth

◦ Vacuum shelves monthly with a HEPA-filter vacuum

◦ Wipe shelves with a slightly damp cloth quarterly

◦ Consider wearing a dust mask while cleaning

2. Protective Measures:

◦ Use glass-front bookcases when possible

◦ Keep books in closed cabinets in humid areas

◦ Use book covers for frequently handled volumes

◦ Place air purifiers near large book collections

James, age 78, found a clever solution: "I keep my most-used books in a glass-front cabinet. They stay clean, and I can see exactly what I have."

Fall Prevention: The Essential Guide

Falls are a serious concern for seniors, and book storage can either help or hinder your safety. Here's how to create a safer environment:

High-Risk Activities to Avoid

1. Reaching Overhead:

◦ Never store frequently used books above shoulder height

◦ Avoid using stepladders or chairs to reach books

◦ Keep heavy books at waist level or lower

2. Bending Low:

◦ Minimize storage of books near floor level

◦ Avoid deep bookshelves that require reaching far back

◦ Don't stack books on the floor

3. Carrying Too Many:

◦ Move books one or two at a time

◦ Use a rolling cart for multiple books

◦ Ask for help with heavy books or large quantities

Creating Safe Spaces

1. Clear Pathways:

◦ Maintain at least 3 feet of clear space between furniture

◦ Remove book stacks from walking areas

◦ Ensure good lighting near bookshelves

◦ Install handrails near reading areas

2. Smart Storage:

◦ Use bookcases with adjustable shelves

◦ Install pullout shelves for easier access

◦ Consider horizontal storage for large books

○ Add lips to shelves to prevent books from falling

Helen, age 85, redesigned her reading space: "I moved my favorite books to a small bookcase next to my chair. Now I don't have to get up and down so much, and everything I need is within easy reach."

Organizing for Accessibility

The key to a safe book collection is organizing it around your current needs and abilities. Here's how to make your books more accessible:

The Comfort Zone Concept

Think of your space in terms of three zones:

1. Easy Access Zone (waist to shoulder height)

○ Everyday books

○ Current reading

○ Frequently referenced materials

2. Secondary Access Zone (knee to waist height)

○ Less frequently used books

○ Heavier volumes

○ Seasonal reading

3. Limited Access Zone (above shoulder or below knee)

○ Archived materials

○ Books kept for sentimental reasons

○ Items rarely accessed

Practical Organization Tips

1. Categorize by Use:

○ Daily use: Keep at easy reach

○ Weekly use: Place in secondary zone

○ Occasional use: Can go in limited access areas

○ Never use: Consider removing

2. Size Considerations:

○ Large, heavy books: Store at waist height

○ Lightweight paperbacks: Can go higher

○ Reference books: Keep where you use them

3. Reading Location:

○ Bedside books: Small, lightweight selections

○ Living room: Current reading within arm's reach

◦ Study: Reference materials at desk height

Barbara, age 76, shares her system: "I keep three books maximum on my nightstand, rotated weekly from my 'current reading' shelf in the living room. Everything else stays organized on shelves, so I'm never tempted to stack books where they might cause problems."

Making Your Space Work for You
Adaptive Solutions

1. Reading Areas:

◦ Place comfortable, sturdy seating near bookshelves

◦ Ensure good lighting from multiple angles

◦ Keep reading glasses and bookmarks within reach

◦ Use book stands for heavy volumes

2. Storage Solutions:

◦ Install pullout shelves for deeper storage

◦ Use bookends to prevent sliding

◦ Consider vertical dividers for paperbacks

◦ Label shelves clearly for easy location

3. Handling Solutions:

◦ Keep a lightweight step stool with handrail for occasional reaching

◦ Use a grabber tool for high shelves

◦ Maintain a small cart for moving books

◦ Keep cleaning supplies easily accessible

Signs You Need to Make Changes

Watch for these warning signs that your book collection needs attention:

1. Physical Indicators:

◦ Difficulty breathing while dusting

◦ Sneezing or coughing near books

◦ Strain while reaching for books

◦ Balance issues while shelving

2. Space Issues:

◦ Books stacked on floors

◦ Crowded shelves that make books hard to remove

◦ Blocked pathways

◦ Dusty books you can't reach to clean

3. Usage Problems:

◦ Can't find books when needed

◦ Avoiding certain shelves due to access difficulties

◦ Books falling when pulled out

◦ Difficulty returning books to proper places

Taking Action: Your Safety Checklist

Use this checklist to evaluate your book storage:

• All frequently used books are between waist and shoulder height

• No books are stored where they require a ladder to reach

• Pathways between bookcases are clear and well-lit

• Heavy books are stored at waist height or lower

• Books are easy to remove and replace on shelves

• Regular cleaning is possible without strain

• No books are stored directly on the floor

• Reading areas have sturdy seating and good lighting

• Book storage is away from humid areas

• Emergency exits are clear of book storage

Chapter Summary

• Book storage safety becomes increasingly important as we age

• Dust and air quality from books can affect health

• Proper organization can prevent falls and strain

• Accessibility should guide book placement decisions

• Regular maintenance is essential for safety

Action Steps

1. This Week:

◦ Identify any immediate safety hazards

◦ Move essential books to easy access zones

◦ Clear all walking paths

2. This Month:

◦ Reorganize books by usage frequency

◦ Set up a cleaning schedule

◦ Create dedicated reading areas

3. Long Term:

◦ Consider installing better storage solutions

○ Develop a maintenance routine

○ Regular safety evaluations

Reflection Questions

Before moving to the next chapter, consider:

1. Which areas of your book storage currently pose risks?

2. What immediate changes could make your books more accessible?

3. How can you make cleaning and maintenance easier?

4. What support might you need to make these changes?

Remember, maintaining a book collection shouldn't put your health at risk. Small changes in how you store and handle your books can make a big difference in your safety and enjoyment of them.

The Digital Revolution

When Alice's arthritis made it difficult to hold heavy books, she thought her reading days might be over. "I couldn't manage the big hardcovers anymore, and even paperbacks were becoming difficult to keep open," she recalls. Then her granddaughter introduced her to an e-reader. "Now I read more than ever. I can make the text as large as I need, and the device is lighter than a magazine."

Why Consider Digital Reading?

Many seniors hesitate to try e-readers, and that's perfectly natural. After all, we've spent decades enjoying traditional books. But digital reading offers solutions to many challenges that come with aging:

Physical Benefits
- Lightweight devices are easier to hold than heavy books
- No need to struggle with small print
- Built-in lighting means no extra reading lamps
- No more wrestling with heavy hardcovers or floppy paperbacks

Practical Advantages
- Thousands of books in one small device
- Many libraries offer free e-book borrowing
- Instant access to new books without leaving home

• Most books cost less in digital format

• No more storage space concerns

Understanding E-Readers: A Simple Guide

Let's look at the main types of devices you can use for digital reading:

Dedicated E-Readers

These devices are designed specifically for reading. The most popular ones use "e-ink" technology, which looks very similar to printed paper.

Benefits:

• Easy on the eyes - no glare or eye strain

• Long battery life (weeks, not hours)

• Works well in bright sunlight

• Simple to use - focused on reading only

• Lightweight and portable

Example: John, age 79, chose a basic e-reader because he wanted something simple. "I just wanted to read books. I didn't need all the extra features of a tablet. The battery lasts forever, and it's so easy to use."

Tablets

Tablets like iPads can be used for reading plus many other activities.

Benefits:

• Color displays for magazines and cookbooks

• Can also be used for email, web browsing, and video calls

• Good for both books and multimedia content

• Usually have larger screens

Margaret, age 75, prefers her tablet: "I use it for reading, but I also like that I can video chat with my grandchildren and look up recipes. It's like having a whole entertainment center in one device."

Making Reading Easier: Digital Features That Help

Digital devices offer many features that can make reading more enjoyable as we age:

Adjustable Text Size

This is perhaps the most important feature for seniors. Instead of searching for large-print editions, you can make ANY book large print.

How it works:
- Most devices offer 6-12 different text sizes
- You can change size at any time while reading
- No need to buy special large-print editions
- Can adjust size depending on time of day or fatigue level

Betty, age 82, shares: "My eyes get tired in the evening, so I make the text larger. In the morning, I can read smaller print. It's wonderful to have that flexibility."

Lighting Options

Built-in lighting means no more struggling with reading lamps or poor lighting.

Features:
- Adjustable brightness for any situation
- Night mode for reading in bed
- No glare in sunlight (on e-ink devices)
- Some devices automatically adjust to room lighting

Font Choices

Different fonts can make reading easier for different people.

Options:
- Choose fonts designed for easier reading
- Adjust spacing between lines
- Change margins for comfort
- Select bold text if needed

Additional Helpful Features

- Dictionary: Tap a word to see its definition
- Bookmarks: Easy to mark and find favorite passages
- Notes: Add thoughts without writing in books
- Search: Find specific words or passages instantly
- Adjustable contrast for better visibility

Getting Started with Digital Reading

If you're interested in trying digital reading, here's a step-by-step approach:

1. Choose the Right Device

Start by considering what matters most to you:

- Simple reading only? Consider a basic e-reader
- Want more features? Look at tablets
- Need very large print? Check screen sizes
- Plan to read outdoors? E-ink might be best

2. Start Small

Begin with one or two books and learn the basic features:

- How to turn pages
- Adjusting text size
- Using the built-in light
- Downloading new books

Rose, age 77, shares her experience: "I started with just one book. My son helped me set it up, and I practiced until I felt comfortable. Now I can do everything myself."

3. Explore Library Options

Most public libraries offer free e-book lending:

- Get a library card if you don't have one
- Ask about digital lending programs
- See if your library offers tech help
- Learn how to borrow and return digital books

4. Build Confidence Gradually

- Practice basic features before trying advanced ones
- Keep instructions handy
- Don't hesitate to ask for help
- Join a digital reading group for seniors

Transitioning Favorite Books to Digital

Many seniors worry about giving up their physical books. Here's how to make a comfortable transition:

Start with New Purchases

- Buy new books in digital format
- Keep existing physical books you love
- Gradually explore digital versions of favorites

Consider Which Books to Transition

Good candidates for digital copies:

- Large, heavy books
- Books with small print
- Books you re-read often

• Reference books you need to search

• Series that take up lots of space

Not everything needs to go digital:

• Special editions

• Signed copies

• Photo books

• Family heirlooms

• Books with sentimental value

David, age 84, found a good balance: "I kept my signed first editions and family Bibles, but moved my mystery collection to digital. Now I have the best of both worlds."

Keeping Cherished Books While Embracing Technology

You don't have to choose between traditional and digital books. Here's how to enjoy both:

Create a Hybrid Library

1 Keep Special Physical Books:

◦ Books with personal inscriptions

◦ Family heirlooms

◦ Beautiful editions you love to display

◦ Books with your notes and memories

2 Go Digital For:

◦ New purchases

◦ Reading copies of favorites

◦ Travel reading

◦ Nighttime reading

◦ Large reference works

Organizing Your Digital Library

Tips for keeping track of digital books:

• Create collections by genre

• Use wishlists for books to read later

• Make a favorites collection

• Keep a reading journal

Helen, age 80, explains her system: "I have my special books on display in the living room, but my everyday reading is all digital now. I love having my whole mystery collection with me wherever

I go."

Common Concerns and Solutions

"I'm worried about technology"

Solution: Start simple with a basic e-reader and just a few books. Many libraries and senior centers offer classes or one-on-one help.

"I'll miss the feel of real books"

Solution: Keep your special books while using digital for everyday reading. You might find you enjoy both for different purposes.

"What if I lose all my books?"

Solution: Digital books are stored in your account, not just on your device. They can't be lost or damaged.

"It seems expensive"

Solution: While devices have an upfront cost, digital books often cost less, and many are free through libraries.

Making the Decision

Consider trying digital reading if you:

• Struggle with book weight or print size
• Want to read in bed without disturbing others
• Need more storage space
• Like to take books when traveling
• Want access to a wider selection of books

Chapter Summary

• Digital reading offers many benefits for seniors
• Various devices suit different needs and preferences
• Features like adjustable text make reading easier
• You can keep special books while enjoying digital convenience
• Starting slowly helps build confidence

Action Steps

1. This Week:

○ Visit your library to learn about digital options
○ Ask family members about their digital reading experience
○ Consider which books you might prefer in digital format

2. This Month:

○ Try a friend's or family member's device
○ Research which type of device might suit you

◦ Make a list of books you'd like in digital format

3. Long Term:

◦ Start building your digital library

◦ Join online reading communities

◦ Share your experience with other seniors

Reflection Questions

Before moving to the next chapter, consider:

1. What challenges with physical books might digital reading solve for you?

2. Which books would you keep in physical form?

3. What support would you need to try digital reading?

4. How might digital reading help you continue enjoying books as you age?

Remember, digital reading isn't about replacing your beloved books – it's about adding new ways to enjoy reading that might be easier and more comfortable as you age

Creating Your Literary Legacy

When William passed away at 89, his family discovered something remarkable. Inside his favorite books, he had left notes about why each one mattered to him. "Finding Dad's notes was like having one last conversation with him," his daughter shared. "Through his books and stories, he's still teaching us things we never knew about his life."

Your books aren't just possessions – they're windows into your life story. This chapter will help you create a meaningful legacy through your books, ensuring that the stories behind them live on.

Why Create a Literary Legacy?

Before we dive into the how-to, let's understand why this matters:

• Books tell the story of your interests and values

• Personal notes make books more meaningful to future generations

• Your reading history offers insights into your life journey

• Thoughtfully shared books create lasting connections

• Stories behind books often get lost if not recorded

Choosing Books to Pass Down

Not every book needs to become a family heirloom. Here's how to select books that will be meaningful to future generations.

What Makes a Book Heritage-Worthy?

1. Personal Connection:
- Books that changed your life
- Books that remind you of important moments
- Books that reflect your values
- Books that taught you crucial lessons

2. Family Significance:
- Books passed down from previous generations
- Books that tell family stories
- Books that reflect family heritage
- Books with family member inscriptions

3. Historical Value:
- Books that capture important times in your life
- Books that document family or local history
- Books that show how times have changed
- First editions or special collections

Eleanor, age 85, shares her approach: "I created small collections for each grandchild based on their interests. For my granddaughter who loves art, I saved my collection of art books and included notes about the galleries I visited and artists I met."

Making Thoughtful Selections

Consider these questions for each book:

1. Why is this book special to me?
2. Who in my family would appreciate it most?
3. What story does this book tell about our family?
4. How might this book be meaningful generations from now?

Recording Stories Behind Special Books

The real value often lies not in the book itself, but in its story. Here's how to preserve these precious memories.

Methods for Recording Book Stories

1. Book Notes:
- Write directly on blank pages (if appropriate)
- Use archival quality paper inserts

- Create separate notebooks with references
- Make digital records

2. What to Include:

- When and where you got the book
- Why it's significant to you
- Special memories associated with it
- Life lessons it taught you
- Historical context from your life

Robert, age 92, found a creative solution: "I recorded short videos about my most special books. I show the book, tell its story, and share why it matters. My great-grandchildren will be able to hear these stories in my own voice."

Sample Book Story Template

Title: Date Acquired: Why This Book Matters: Special Memories: Life Lessons: Why I'm Passing It On: Who Might Appreciate It Most:

Creating a Family Library

A family library is more than just a collection of books – it's a curated selection that tells your family's story.

Organizing Your Family Library

1. Physical Organization:

- Group books by family connection
- Create sections for different generations
- Include family photos with relevant books
- Make space for future additions

2. Documentation:

- Catalog special books
- Create a family reading history
- Map book connections to family events
- Record care instructions

Margaret, age 88, developed a unique system: "I created 'family reading boxes' for each branch of our family. Each box contains books that connect to that part of the family's history, along with notes explaining the connections."

Making It Accessible

Tips for creating an accessible family library:

1. Clear labeling
2. Easy-to-follow organization
3. Protection for fragile items
4. Digital backup of important information
5. Instructions for maintenance

Documenting Your Reading History

Your reading journey tells the story of your life. Here's how to preserve it.

Creating a Reading Timeline

1. Childhood Books:

◦ First books you remember
◦ Books that sparked interests
◦ School reading that influenced you
◦ Gifts that made an impact

2. Young Adult Years:

◦ Books that shaped your beliefs
◦ Professional development reading
◦ Books shared with friends
◦ Books that guided major decisions

3. Adult Life:

◦ Books that helped in parenting
◦ Career-influencing reading
◦ Books that helped in hard times
◦ Books that brought joy

4. Later Years:

◦ Books that gained new meaning
◦ Reading that connected generations
◦ Books that provided perspective
◦ Current favorites

James, age 86, shares his method: "I created a 'Book of Books' – a journal where I write about the books that marked important moments in my life. Each entry includes when I read it, why it mattered then, and what it means to me now."

Recording Methods

1. Written Documentation:
◦ Reading journals
◦ Book lists with notes
◦ Timeline format
◦ Narrative style

2. Digital Options:
◦ Spreadsheets
◦ Digital journals
◦ Audio recordings
◦ Video memories

3. Creative Approaches:
◦ Scrapbooks with book covers
◦ Photo albums of reading moments
◦ Family reading trees
◦ Reading maps showing where you read special books

Making It Meaningful for Future Generations
Connecting Books to Family Stories

1. Create Context:
◦ Link books to family events
◦ Explain historical connections
◦ Share personal insights
◦ Connect to family values

2. Add Personal Touches:
◦ Include photos of you reading the book
◦ Save relevant bookmarks
◦ Keep related letters or cards
◦ Note special occasions when the book was read

Helen, age 90, made it personal: "In my cookbook collection, I noted which recipes we used for family celebrations, who loved what dishes, and how recipes evolved with our family traditions."

Preservation Tips

1. Physical Care:
◦ Use acid-free boxes
◦ Store away from direct sunlight
◦ Control humidity
◦ Handle with clean, dry hands

2. Information Preservation:
◦ Make digital copies of notes
◦ Record verbal histories
◦ Create backup documentation
◦ Share information with multiple family members

Special Projects to Consider

Family Reading Album

Create a special album that includes:

1. Photos of family reading moments
2. Notes about favorite books
3. Reading traditions
4. Special reading places
5. Book-related memories

Reading Legacy Letter

Write a letter to future generations about:

1. How books shaped your life
2. What reading means to you
3. Wisdom found in favorite books
4. Hopes for future readers

Family Book Map

Create a visual representation of:

1. Books passed through generations
2. Where family books came from
3. Reading connections between family members
4. Future book destinations

Common Challenges and Solutions

"No One Seems Interested"

Solution: Start small, focus on quality over quantity, and connect books to family stories.

"Too Much to Document"

Solution: Begin with the most special books and add others as time permits.

"Don't Know Where to Start"

Solution: Start with one special book and let the process grow naturally.

"Worried About Fairness"

Solution: Focus on matching books to interests rather than equal numbers.

Success Stories

Martha, age 87: "I created reading boxes for each grandchild, filling them with books that connected to their interests and our family history. Now they're doing the same for their children."

Thomas, age 92: "I recorded the story of each book in my father's collection, sharing memories of him reading them to me. My great-grandchildren now know their great-great-grandfather through these stories."

Chapter Summary
- Literary legacies connect generations through books
- Personal stories make books more meaningful
- Documentation preserves memories
- Organization makes legacy accessible
- Different methods suit different needs

Action Steps

1 This Week:
- Choose one special book to document
- Start a simple reading journal
- Take photos of favorite books
- Make initial family book lists

2 This Month:
- Create basic documentation system
- Record stories for most special books
- Contact family about interests
- Start organizing family library

3 Long Term:
- Complete documentation
- Create preservation system
- Share stories with family
- Plan future distribution

Reflection Questions

Before moving to the next chapter, consider:

1. Which books tell important parts of your story?

2. What reading memories do you want to preserve?

3. How can you make your literary legacy meaningful?

4. What support might you need to complete this project?

Remember: Your literary legacy is about more than just books — it's about sharing your life story, values, and wisdom with future generations.

Practical Solutions for Storage

When Barbara couldn't reach her favorite cookbooks anymore, her son noticed she had stopped cooking the family recipes she loved. "I just couldn't manage those heavy books on the top shelf," she explained. After reorganizing her cookbooks to a lower cabinet with pull-out shelves, she started cooking again. Sometimes the simplest changes make the biggest difference.

Understanding Your Storage Needs

Before we explore specific solutions, let's think about what makes book storage work for seniors:

- Easy access without stretching or bending
- Books organized by how often you use them
- Clear visibility of book spines
- Safe and stable storage systems
- Easy cleaning and maintenance

Organizing by Accessibility Needs

The Three-Zone System

Think of your storage space in three zones:

1. Prime Zone (Waist to Shoulder Height):
○ Books you read regularly
○ Current reading materials

- Frequently referenced books
- Lighter weight books
- Books with larger print

2. Secondary Zone (Mid-Thigh to Waist):

- Heavier books you use occasionally
- Photo albums and larger books
- Seasonal reading materials
- Reference books used monthly

3. Storage Zone (Below Mid-Thigh or Above Shoulder):

- Books kept for sentimental reasons
- Rarely used references
- Books being saved for family
- Archive materials

Thomas, age 84, shares his experience: "I moved all my mystery novels to the middle shelves where I can easily reach them while sitting in my reading chair. Now I read more because it's not a struggle to get the books."

Practical Organization Tips

1. Frequency of Use:

- Daily use: Prime zone
- Weekly use: Upper secondary zone
- Monthly use: Lower secondary zone
- Rarely used: Storage zone

2. Physical Considerations:

- Heavy books: Waist height or lower
- Small print books: Prime zone for better light
- Frequently cleaned books: Easy-reach zones
- Delicate books: Protected areas

Creative Storage Solutions for Limited Mobility

Accessible Bookcase Alternatives

1. Rolling Book Carts:

- Move books where you need them
- Adjustable heights available
- Can serve as side tables
- Easy to clean around

2. Revolving Bookcases:

- Access books from multiple sides
- Reduce need to reach or bend
- Good for corner spaces
- Can be mounted at ideal height

3. Pull-Out Shelves:

- Bring books forward for easy access
- Reduce reaching and bending
- Work well in deep cabinets
- Can be added to existing shelves

Margaret, age 79, found an innovative solution: "I converted an old TV cabinet into a book cabinet with pull-out shelves. I can sit in my chair and roll out exactly what I want to read."

Small Space Solutions

1. Vertical Storage:

- Door-mounted racks
- Over-chair bookcases
- Window-seat storage
- Behind-furniture shelving

2. Furniture with Built-in Storage:

- Reading chairs with book pockets
- Ottoman storage
- Bedside tables with shelves
- End tables with book compartments

Adaptive Equipment

1. Book Retrieval Tools:

- Reaching tools with rubber grips
- Book hooks for high shelves
- Sliding book supports
- Wheeled step stools with handles

2. Reading Supports:

- Adjustable book stands
- Lap desks with book holders
- Page holders
- Book weights

Robert, age 88, uses several aids: "I have a reaching tool for higher shelves and a book stand that holds my heavy art books. These simple tools help me stay independent with my reading."

Maintaining a Clean and Organized Collection
Easy-Clean Storage Solutions

1. Dust-Resistant Options:
- Glass-front cabinets
- Sliding doors
- Book covers
- Protective sleeves

2. Easy-Access Cleaning:
- Open shelving at reachable heights
- Space between books for dusting
- Smooth surfaces that wipe clean
- Removable shelf liners

Organization Systems

1. Clear Labeling:
- Large print labels
- Color coding
- Category markers
- Shelf tags

2. Logical Arrangements:
- Books grouped by topic
- Size-based organization
- Color coordination
- Alphabetical when practical

Helen, age 82, developed a simple system: "I use different colored stickers on the spine – red for mysteries, blue for history, green for nature books. I can find what I want at a glance."

Regular Maintenance Schedule

1. Daily Tasks:
- Return books to proper places
- Keep frequently used areas clear
- Wipe visible dust
- Check for stability

2. Weekly Tasks:
- Basic dusting

- Organize current reading area
- Check book conditions
- Adjust books for easy access

3. Monthly Tasks:
- Deep clean accessible shelves
- Rotate seasonal books
- Check for damage
- Update organization system

Adapting Bookshelves for Senior-Friendly Use

Physical Modifications

1. Height Adjustments:
- Lower tall bookcases
- Raise bottom shelves
- Install adjustable shelving
- Create reachable zones

2. Depth Modifications:
- Add pull-out runners
- Install sliding shelves
- Create two-tier systems
- Use shelf extenders

3. Safety Features:
- Secure bookcases to walls
- Install sturdy handles
- Add non-slip shelf liners
- Provide adequate lighting

James, age 86, made smart changes: "I added motion-sensor lights above my bookcases and installed pull-out shelves. Now I can see and reach everything safely."

Lighting Solutions

1. Built-in Options:
- Under-shelf lighting
- Battery-operated shelf lights
- Motion-activated systems
- Adjustable book lights

2. Ambient Lighting:
- Reading lamps near shelves

- Wall sconces
- Ceiling spots
- Natural light positioning

Comfort Features

1. Seating Arrangements:
- Reading chairs near shelves
- Small stools for lower access
- Support rails near bookcases
- Rest spots between shelves

2. Access Tools:
- Book retrieval hooks
- Extending grab tools
- Mobile steps with railings
- Book support stands

Making It Work in Different Spaces

Small Apartments

1. Space-Saving Ideas:
- Corner bookcases
- Over-door storage
- Furniture with hidden storage
- Vertical space utilization

2. Multi-Purpose Solutions:
- Room divider bookcases
- Storage ottomans
- Reading nook creation
- Window seat storage

Larger Homes

1. Reading Room Setup:
- Central seating area
- Surrounding accessible shelves
- Good natural light
- Multiple access points

2. Distributed Storage:
- Topic-based locations
- Activity-centered placement
- Seasonal rotation areas

◦ Archive spaces

Common Challenges and Solutions

Limited Reach

Solution: Install pull-out shelves and use reaching tools

Heavy Books

Solution: Store at waist height and use book stands

Poor Lighting

Solution: Add dedicated shelf lighting and position near windows

Difficult Navigation

Solution: Create clear pathways and add support rails

Success Stories

Mary, age 90: "I converted my rarely-used dining room into a reading room with low bookcases all around. Now I can reach everything while sitting in my comfortable chair."

David, age 85: "Installing pull-out shelves changed everything. I can bring the books to me instead of reaching for them."

Chapter Summary

- Organization should prioritize accessibility
- Creative solutions can overcome mobility limitations
- Regular maintenance keeps collections manageable
- Proper adaptations enhance safety and enjoyment

Action Steps

1. This Week:

◦ Evaluate current storage setup

◦ Identify problem areas

◦ List frequently used books

◦ Check lighting conditions

2. This Month:

◦ Reorganize books by accessibility

◦ Install basic safety features

◦ Set up cleaning schedule

◦ Add necessary lighting

3. Long Term:

◦ Make structural modifications

◦ Install adaptive equipment

  ○ Create maintenance routine

  ○ Update as needs change

Reflection Questions

Before moving to the next chapter, consider:

1. Which books do you need most accessible?

2. What storage challenges frustrate you most?

3. What safety features would help you?

4. How can you make maintenance easier?

Remember: Good storage solutions should make your books more accessible and enjoyable while keeping you safe and comfortable.

The Joy of Sharing

When Eleanor decided to share her collection of children's books, she didn't just drop them off at the local library. Instead, she sat with her grandchildren, telling them stories about each book — which ones their parents loved, which ones taught her important lessons, and which ones made everyone laugh. "Now these books have new life," she says. "They're not just sitting on a shelf; they're creating new memories."

Why Sharing Books Matters

Books have a unique power to connect people. When we share books thoughtfully, we:

- Keep stories and ideas alive
- Help others discover new worlds
- Create meaningful connections
- Build community bonds
- Save resources by reusing books

Finding New Homes for Beloved Books

Not all books should go to the same place. Different books need different homes where they'll be most appreciated and useful.

Matching Books to Recipients

1. Educational Books:

- Schools and teachers
- Adult education programs
- Literacy programs
- Student organizations

2. Professional Books:
- Training programs
- Career centers
- Professional associations
- Business incubators

3. Special Interest Books:
- Hobby groups
- Community centers
- Special interest clubs
- Learning centers

Robert, age 82, found the perfect home for his engineering books: "I donated my technical library to a community college. Now students who can't afford expensive textbooks can use them. The instructor tells me they're always being borrowed."

Making Meaningful Donations

Before donating, consider:

1. Book condition
2. Current relevance
3. Potential user needs
4. Accessibility of location
5. Organization's requirements

Tips for successful donation:

- Call ahead to confirm acceptance
- Clean and check books
- Pack similar books together
- Include notes about special features
- Offer additional context if valuable

Contributing to Community Libraries

Libraries serve as community hubs, and thoughtful donations can make a real difference.

Understanding Library Needs

1. Public Libraries:

- Popular fiction in good condition
- Current non-fiction
- Local history materials
- Large print books
- Children's books

2. Special Libraries:

- Topic-specific collections
- Research materials
- Historical documents
- Specialized references

Margaret, age 78, made a special contribution: "I had a collection of local history books with notes about our town's development. The library created a special local history section with them."

Making Library Donations Count

1. Preparation Steps:

- Check library guidelines
- Sort by category
- Remove personal items
- Clean thoroughly
- Document any special features

2. Special Considerations:

- Rare or valuable books
- Local interest items
- Complete series
- Special editions
- Signed copies

Beyond Basic Donations

Consider these additional ways to help:

1. Volunteer to organize books
2. Share stories about special books
3. Help with book sales
4. Join Friends of the Library
5. Support reading programs

Teaching Grandchildren About Your Favorite Books

Sharing books with grandchildren creates lasting bonds and passes on family history.

Creating Reading Connections

1. Story Sharing Sessions:

◦ Read together regularly

◦ Share book memories

◦ Discuss lessons learned

◦ Connect books to family stories

◦ Create reading traditions

2. Special Book Activities:

◦ Book-based crafts

◦ Story-inspired games

◦ Reading journals

◦ Character discussions

◦ Book-themed gatherings

Helen, age 85, created a special tradition: "Every Sunday, I read with my grandchildren over video chat. We pick books that I loved reading to their parents, and I tell them stories about when their mom or dad was little."

Making Books Come Alive

1. Interactive Reading:

◦ Ask questions

◦ Make predictions

◦ Share personal connections

◦ Create voices for characters

◦ Discuss illustrations

2. Extended Activities:

◦ Draw favorite scenes

◦ Write alternate endings

◦ Act out stories

◦ Make book-inspired meals

◦ Create story collections

Building Reading Traditions

1. Regular Reading Times:

◦ Weekly story hours

◦ Holiday book sharing

◦ Birthday book traditions

◦ Summer reading clubs

○ Family book discussions

2. Special Book Events:

○ Book-themed parties

○ Reading challenges

○ Story creation sessions

○ Book character days

○ Family reading nights

Building Connections Through Book Donations

Book sharing can create unexpected connections and communities.

Finding Sharing Opportunities

1. Local Organizations:

○ Senior centers

○ Community centers

○ Religious organizations

○ Youth programs

○ Cultural centers

2. Special Programs:

○ Prison libraries

○ Military bases

○ Homeless shelters

○ Women's shelters

○ Children's hospitals

Thomas, age 89, discovered an unexpected connection: "I donated my mystery collection to the senior center. Now there's a weekly mystery book club, and I've made new friends who love the same authors I do."

Creating Sharing Programs

1. Book Exchange Programs:

○ Neighborhood book swaps

○ Genre-specific exchanges

○ Reading circles

○ Book rotation groups

○ Seasonal book sharing

2. Reading Communities:

○ Book discussion groups

- Reading buddies
- Story sharing circles
- Author appreciation clubs
- Genre interest groups

Making Lasting Impacts

1. Educational Support:

- School reading programs
- Literacy initiatives
- Language learning groups
- Tutorial programs
- Special education resources

2. Community Building:

- Multi-generational book clubs
- Cultural exchange programs
- Reading mentorship
- Literary events
- Book festivals

Special Projects to Consider

Creating Reading Legacy Projects

1. Family Reading History:

- Document favorite books
- Record reading memories
- Create book timelines
- Share reading traditions
- Map book journeys

2. Community Reading Initiatives:

- Start little free libraries
- Organize book drives
- Create reading groups
- Support literacy programs
- Develop book sharing systems

Sarah, age 80, started something special: "I helped set up a 'Grandparents' Favorites' shelf at our library. Seniors donate books they loved reading to their children, along with notes about why these books are special."

Success Stories

Mary, age 87: "I donated my teaching books to a new teacher. She says she uses them every day, and sometimes calls me for advice. It's wonderful to know my life's work is still helping others."

James, age 92: "I started reading my adventure books with my great-grandson over video chat. Now he wants to be an explorer, just like I did at his age."

Common Challenges and Solutions

"Books Might Not Be Wanted"

Solution: Research organizations' needs and match books accordingly

"Don't Know Where to Start"

Solution: Begin with one category or one organization

"Worried About Condition"

Solution: Sort by condition and be honest about book quality

"Transportation Issues"

Solution: Ask about pickup services or coordinate with family

Chapter Summary

• Thoughtful sharing extends books' impact

• Different books need different homes

• Sharing creates connections

• Teaching through books builds legacy

• Community building through books

Action Steps

1. This Week:

◦ Sort books by potential recipients

◦ Research local donation options

◦ Contact family about book interests

◦ Plan reading sessions

2. This Month:

◦ Begin donation process

◦ Start reading traditions

◦ Join or create book groups

◦ Document special books

3. Long Term:

◦ Develop sharing systems

◦ Build reading communities

- Create lasting traditions
- Monitor impact

Reflection Questions

Before moving to the next chapter, consider:

1. Which books could benefit others most?
2. What reading traditions do you want to start?
3. How can your books serve your community?
4. What stories do you want to share?

Remember: Sharing books thoughtfully creates connections, preserves memories, and builds communities while giving your beloved books new life with appreciative readers.

Maintaining Your Curated Collection

After spending months organizing her books, Martha faced a new challenge. "I had everything perfectly arranged," she says, "but within six months, new books started piling up, and I was back to feeling overwhelmed." Like many seniors, Martha learned that maintaining an organized collection is just as important as creating one.

Creating a Sustainable System

A sustainable system means your book collection stays manageable without constant effort. Think of it like tending a garden – regular small efforts prevent big problems.

Foundation of a Sustainable System

1. Designated Spaces:
◦ Every book needs a proper home
◦ Allow room for growth
◦ Keep frequently used books accessible
◦ Create temporary spaces for new arrivals

2. Clear Categories:
◦ Current reading
◦ Reference books

- Seasonal books
- Special collections
- Family heritage books

Robert, age 84, shares his approach: "I divided my shelves into zones – current reading near my chair, reference books in the study, and seasonal books in the guest room closet. When I get a new book, I know exactly where it should go."

Setting Up Your System

1. Physical Organization:
- Label shelves clearly
- Use bookends for stability
- Leave space for adjustments
- Create easy-access areas

2. Documentation:
- Simple catalog system
- Reading log
- Maintenance schedule
- Cleaning routine

3. Decision Guidelines:
- What to keep
- When to pass along
- How to store
- When to rotate

The One-In-One-Out Rule

This simple rule helps prevent overcrowding and ensures your collection stays manageable.

How It Works

For every new book that enters your collection:

1. One book must leave through:
- Donation
- Passing to family
- Selling
- Recycling

Helen, age 79, made it work for her: "When I get a new mystery novel, I choose one from my existing collection to donate to the senior center. This keeps my collection fresh without overwhelming my space."

Making the Rule Work for You

1. Exceptions to Consider:
◦ Special editions
◦ Family heirlooms
◦ Irreplaceable books
◦ Reference sets

2. Decision Questions:
◦ Which book brings more value?
◦ Which fits better in my space?
◦ Which do I use more?
◦ Which serves my current needs?

Practical Application

1. New Book Process:
◦ Evaluate new acquisition
◦ Review similar books
◦ Choose one to remove
◦ Process removed book appropriately

2. Category Management:
◦ Keep genre sections balanced
◦ Maintain accessibility
◦ Consider space limitations
◦ Preserve special collections

Regular Maintenance and Cleaning

Clean, well-maintained books last longer and are more enjoyable to use. Here's how to keep your collection in good condition without overwhelming yourself.

Daily Care

1. Basic Tasks:
◦ Return books to proper places
◦ Dust visible surfaces
◦ Check for damage
◦ Maintain clear spaces

2. Reading Area Care:

- Clean reading surfaces
- Organize current books
- Check lighting
- Clear pathways

Thomas, age 88, developed an easy routine: "Every evening before bed, I return the books I used that day to their shelves. It takes five minutes but keeps everything organized."

Weekly Maintenance

1. Cleaning Tasks:
- Dust accessible shelves
- Wipe book covers
- Clean reading glasses
- Check book supports

2. Organization Tasks:
- Sort current reading
- Update reading log
- Check new acquisitions
- Plan donations

Monthly Deep Care

1. Thorough Cleaning:
- Complete shelf dusting
- Book cover cleaning
- Bookend wiping
- Environmental check

2. Collection Review:
- Check for damage
- Evaluate arrangements
- Plan rotations
- Update documentation

Margaret, age 82, shares her system: "The first Sunday of each month, I spend two hours caring for my books. I dust thoroughly, check for problems, and rearrange anything that needs it. This regular attention keeps everything manageable."

Cleaning Methods

1. Safe Cleaning Tools:

- Microfiber cloths
- Soft brushes
- Clean feather dusters
- Book-specific cleaners

2. Cleaning Techniques:
- Wipe away from spines
- Use gentle pressure
- Avoid moisture
- Clean surrounding areas

Seasonal Rotation of Displayed Books

Rotating books seasonally keeps your collection fresh and relevant while managing space effectively.

Planning Seasonal Displays

1. Holiday Books:
- Christmas stories
- Holiday cookbooks
- Seasonal crafts
- Traditional readings

2. Seasonal Reading:
- Summer beach books
- Winter evening novels
- Spring gardening guides
- Fall cooking collections

Barbara, age 85, enjoys her rotation system: "I change my displayed books with the seasons. Winter shows my cozy mysteries and Christmas books, spring brings out my gardening collection, summer features light reading, and fall showcases my cooking books."

Creating Rotation Schedule

1. Quarterly Changes:
- Begin each season
- Plan transitions
- Prepare storage
- Update displays

2. Special Occasions:
- Family visits

- Holidays
- Birthdays
- Anniversaries

Storage for Rotated Books

1. Storage Solutions:
- Clear containers
- Labeled boxes
- Climate-controlled areas
- Accessible storage

2. Organization Methods:
- Group by season
- Label clearly
- Track locations
- Maintain inventory

Special Considerations

Weather Protection

1. Humidity Control:
- Use dehumidifiers
- Check for dampness
- Monitor conditions
- Protect valuable books

2. Temperature Management:
- Avoid direct sunlight
- Maintain steady temperature
- Check problem areas
- Use proper storage

Pest Prevention

1. Regular Checks:
- Look for signs of insects
- Check dark corners
- Monitor storage areas
- Inspect new acquisitions

2. Prevention Methods:
- Keep areas clean
- Use proper storage
- Maintain environment

◦ Act quickly on problems

James, age 86, learned from experience: "I lost some valuable books to moisture damage before I realized my basement storage wasn't suitable. Now I keep everything upstairs and use a dehumidifier."

Maintaining Special Collections
Family Heritage Books

1. Extra Care:
◦ Special cleaning
◦ Careful handling
◦ Proper storage
◦ Regular checks

2. Documentation:
◦ Condition notes
◦ Family history
◦ Care instructions
◦ Future plans

Valuable Books

1. Protection:
◦ Climate control
◦ Special storage
◦ Handling guidelines
◦ Insurance coverage

2. Regular Assessment:
◦ Condition check
◦ Value updates
◦ Storage evaluation
◦ Professional review

Success Stories

Mary, age 90: "I created a simple computer spreadsheet to track my books. When I get something new, I record it and note what I passed along. It helps me maintain balance in my collection."

David, age 87: "By rotating my books seasonally, I enjoy them more and have room to display everything properly. Plus, it's like reuniting with old friends when each season comes around."

Common Challenges and Solutions

"Too Many New Books"

Solution: Use the one-in-one-out rule strictly and consider digital alternatives

"Cleaning Is Difficult"

Solution: Break tasks into small, manageable sessions and use adaptive tools

"Storage Space Issues"

Solution: Rotate books seasonally and use vertical space effectively

"Keeping Track Is Hard"

Solution: Use a simple recording system and regular review schedule

Chapter Summary

- Sustainable systems prevent future problems
- Regular maintenance keeps collections manageable
- Seasonal rotation maximizes space and enjoyment
- Simple rules help maintain organization

Action Steps

1. This Week:
- Create maintenance schedule
- Set up cleaning supplies
- Start tracking system
- Review current arrangement

2. This Month:
- Implement one-in-one-out rule
- Begin regular cleaning routine
- Plan seasonal rotations
- Organize storage areas

3. Long Term:
- Maintain consistent system
- Adjust as needs change
- Review and update methods
- Monitor collection growth

Reflection Questions

Before moving to the next chapter, consider:

1. What aspects of maintenance need most attention?

2. How can you make care routines easier?

3. What seasonal changes would benefit your collection?

4. What support might you need?

Remember: A well-maintained book collection brings joy without becoming a burden. Small, regular efforts keep your books in good condition and your space organized.

Digital Resources and Community

When Joan's eyesight started making reading difficult, she thought her book club days were over. "I couldn't read the small print anymore, and large-print editions weren't always available," she recalls. Then a librarian introduced her to digital books and audiobooks. "Now I not only keep up with my local book club, but I'm also part of an online reading group. I'm reading more than ever."

Library Apps and Online Resources

Today's libraries offer much more than physical books. Understanding these digital resources can open up new worlds of reading.

Your Library Card's Hidden Powers

Most library cards now give you access to:

- Free e-books
- Digital audiobooks
- Online magazines
- Newspapers archives
- Learning courses
- Movie streaming

Robert, age 82, discovered this value: "I had no idea my library card could do so much. Now I download audiobooks for my daily walks and read magazines on my tablet. I haven't spent a penny on reading material in months."

Popular Library Apps

1. Libby (by OverDrive):

◦ Free with library card

◦ Easy to use interface

◦ Adjustable text size

◦ Built-in audiobook player

◦ Automatic returns

2. Hoopla:

◦ Multiple format options

◦ No wait times

◦ Easy browsing

◦ Simple checkout process

◦ Works on most devices

How to Get Started:

1. Visit your local library

2. Get a library card

3. Download the recommended app

4. Enter your card number

5. Start borrowing

Margaret, age 78, shares her experience: "The librarian helped me set up the Libby app on my tablet. Now I can check out books at midnight if I can't sleep!"

Online Reading Resources

1. Project Gutenberg:

◦ Free classic books

◦ Multiple formats

◦ No registration needed

◦ Downloadable content

◦ Vast selection

2. Internet Archive:

◦ Historical materials

◦ Academic resources

◦ Magazine archives

○ Newspaper collections

○ Educational content

Book-Swapping Communities for Seniors

Book swapping gives books new life and helps readers find new treasures without cost.

Online Swapping Platforms

1. BookMooch:

○ Point-based system

○ International community

○ Clear guidelines

○ Active senior members

○ Category browsing

2. PaperBackSwap:

○ Direct exchanges

○ Large selection

○ Member ratings

○ Safe shipping methods

○ Active forums

Helen, age 85, loves her swapping community: "I've exchanged books with people across the country. Each book comes with a note, and I've made several pen pals this way."

Local Swapping Groups

1. Senior Center Exchanges:

○ Regular meetings

○ Social interaction

○ Easy transportation

○ Personal recommendations

○ Community building

2. Neighborhood Book Shares:

○ Little Free Libraries

○ Building book boxes

○ Community shelves

○ Monthly meetups

○ Genre exchanges

Starting Your Own Swap Group

Steps to Success:
1. Find interested members
2. Set clear guidelines
3. Choose meeting place
4. Establish schedule
5. Track exchanges

Thomas, age 79, created a solution: "I started a book swap in our retirement community. We meet monthly in the common room, exchange books, and discuss what we've read. It's become a highlight of our social calendar."

Digital Book Clubs

Online book clubs offer flexibility and community without transportation challenges.

Types of Digital Clubs

1. Video Chat Clubs:
◦ Face-to-face interaction
◦ Scheduled meetings
◦ Social connection
◦ Group discussions
◦ Shared reading plans

2. Forum-Based Clubs:
◦ Flexible participation
◦ Written discussions
◦ Time to reflect
◦ Ongoing conversations
◦ Easy reference

3. Social Media Groups:
◦ Regular interaction
◦ Quick updates
◦ Photo sharing
◦ Reading challenges
◦ Community support

Mary, age 88, found her perfect fit: "I joined a Zoom book club for seniors. We meet twice monthly, and I love seeing everyone's faces. It's like having visitors who love books as much as I do."

Starting a Digital Club

Essential Elements:
1. Clear Schedule:
◦ Regular meeting times
◦ Reading deadlines
◦ Discussion periods
◦ Social time
◦ Special events
2. Structure Guidelines:
◦ Book selection process
◦ Discussion format
◦ Participation rules
◦ Technology help
◦ Backup plans
3. Social Components:
◦ Welcome routines
◦ Personal sharing
◦ Reading memories
◦ Book reactions
◦ Future planning

Accessing Audiobooks and Large-Print Editions
These formats make reading accessible for everyone.
Audiobook Sources
1. Library Services:
◦ Free downloads
◦ Professional narration
◦ Various formats
◦ Multiple devices
◦ Easy playback
2. Commercial Services:
◦ Subscription options
◦ Vast selections
◦ Quality production
◦ Device flexibility
◦ Social features

Barbara, age 92, found freedom in audiobooks: "I listen while I knit, cook, or just rest my eyes. The narrators bring books to life in ways I never expected."

Large-Print Options

1. Digital Solutions:

◦ Adjustable text size

◦ Contrast control

◦ Font choices

◦ Lighting options

◦ Portable convenience

2. Traditional Sources:

◦ Library collections

◦ Publisher series

◦ Special editions

◦ Print-on-demand

◦ Exchange programs

Making the Most of Both

Combined Strategies:

1. Whisper-sync reading:

◦ Switch between formats

◦ Keep your place

◦ Flex with needs

◦ Share devices

◦ Track progress

2. Multi-format approach:

◦ Morning reading

◦ Afternoon listening

◦ Evening digital

◦ Travel options

◦ Social sharing

James, age 86, uses multiple formats: "I read large-print books at home, listen to audiobooks on walks, and use my tablet for bedtime reading. Each format serves a different need."

Success Stories

Sarah, age 90: "I never thought I'd enjoy digital books, but now I read more than ever. I can make the text as large as I need, and I never run out of books."

David, age 87: "Our digital book club has members from across the country. We've learned so much from each other's perspectives and reading experiences."

Common Challenges and Solutions

"Technology Seems Complicated"

Solution: Start with one app and get help setting it up

"Miss Physical Books"

Solution: Combine traditional and digital reading

"Feel Isolated"

Solution: Join online communities and participate regularly

"Hard to Choose Formats"

Solution: Try different options and use what works best for each situation

Chapter Summary

• Digital resources expand reading options
• Online communities provide social connection
• Multiple formats serve different needs
• Technology makes reading more accessible

Action Steps

1. This Week:
◦ Visit library for digital access
◦ Download one reading app
◦ Explore online communities
◦ Try an audiobook

2. This Month:
◦ Join online book group
◦ Start book swapping
◦ Learn new digital tools
◦ Establish reading routine

3. Long Term:
◦ Build digital library
◦ Create reading community
◦ Explore new formats
◦ Share experiences

Reflection Questions

Before moving to the next chapter, consider:

1. Which digital resources interest you most?

2. What type of online community would you enjoy?

3. How could multiple formats enhance your reading?

4. What support do you need to get started?

Remember: Digital resources and communities can enhance your reading life, providing new ways to enjoy books and connect with others.

Living Lighter, Reading Better

Eleanor stood in her newly organized reading room, feeling a sense of peace she hadn't experienced in years. "I used to feel guilty about my crowded bookshelves," she says. "Now each book I keep has a purpose and brings me joy. I'm reading more than ever, but without the weight of books I'll never open again."

The Freedom of a Curated Collection

A curated book collection is like a well-tended garden – every plant has its place and purpose. Understanding this freedom can transform your relationship with books.

What Freedom Looks Like

1. Physical Freedom:
- Clear spaces
- Easy movement
- Accessible books
- Clean surfaces
- Organized shelves

2. Mental Freedom:
- No guilt about unread books
- Clear reading choices
- Purposeful collection

- Meaningful selections
- Reduced overwhelm

Robert, age 84, describes his experience: "After curating my collection, I stopped feeling pressured by all the books I 'should' read. Now I focus on books that truly interest me, and reading is pure pleasure again."

Benefits of Curation

1. Practical Advantages:
- Find books easily
- Clean without struggle
- Access favorites quickly
- Maintain organization
- Share effectively

2. Emotional Benefits:
- Reduced stress
- Increased enjoyment
- Better focus
- Greater appreciation
- Deeper connection

Margaret, age 88, shares her discovery: "With fewer books, I actually read more. Each book in my collection means something special, and I'm no longer distracted by books I'll never read."

Making Space for New Experiences

Physical space often translates to mental space. When we clear our shelves, we open ourselves to new possibilities.

Creating Room for Growth

1. Physical Space:
- Reading nooks
- Discussion areas
- Creative corners
- Learning spaces
- Social gathering spots

2. Mental Space:
- New interests
- Fresh perspectives
- Learning opportunities

◦ Social connections

◦ Creative endeavors

Helen, age 82, found unexpected benefits: "Clearing my overcrowded study made room for a comfortable reading chair and a small table. Now my grandchildren come over for reading time, and we've started a family book club."

Embracing New Possibilities

1. Reading Adventures:

◦ Different genres

◦ New authors

◦ Various formats

◦ Reading groups

◦ Learning programs

2. Social Connections:

◦ Book discussions

◦ Reading partners

◦ Sharing stories

◦ Teaching others

◦ Building community

Making Room for Activities

1. Reading-Related:

◦ Writing groups

◦ Story times

◦ Book crafts

◦ Reading journals

◦ Discussion circles

2. New Hobbies:

◦ Creative writing

◦ Storytelling

◦ Memory recording

◦ Book arts

◦ Reading teaching

Finding Balance Between Old and New

Balance doesn't mean equal parts – it means finding the right mix for your life today.

Maintaining Connections to the Past

1. Heritage Books:
◦ Family histories
◦ Special memories
◦ Important lessons
◦ Cultural connections
◦ Personal landmarks
2. Meaningful Collections:
◦ Curated series
◦ Valued authors
◦ Special editions
◦ Personal favorites
◦ Legacy items

Thomas, age 90, found his balance: "I kept the books that tell my life story – my father's Bible, my children's first books, and the novels that shaped my thinking. Everything else I pass along to others who need them now."

Embracing the Present
1. Current Interests:
◦ New learning
◦ Active hobbies
◦ Present passions
◦ Daily references
◦ Ongoing projects
2. Modern Conveniences:
◦ Digital options
◦ Audio formats
◦ Easy access
◦ Portable reading
◦ Flexible solutions

Building for the Future
1. Legacy Planning:
◦ Family connections
◦ Teaching tools
◦ Shared stories
◦ Future gifts
◦ Lasting impact

2. Adaptable Systems:
◦ Flexible storage
◦ Changing needs
◦ Growing interests
◦ New formats
◦ Evolving collections

Celebrating Your Decluttering Success

Recognizing achievements helps maintain motivation and appreciation for your organized space.

Measuring Success

1. Physical Changes:
◦ Clear spaces
◦ Organized shelves
◦ Clean surfaces
◦ Easy access
◦ Comfortable areas

2. Personal Impact:
◦ Reduced stress
◦ Increased reading
◦ Better focus
◦ More enjoyment
◦ Greater peace

Sarah, age 85, celebrates her achievement: "I took before and after photos of my library. The difference isn't just in how it looks – it's in how I feel when I enter the room. Now it's my favorite place in the house."

Maintaining Success

1. Regular Habits:
◦ Daily tidying
◦ Weekly reviews
◦ Monthly checks
◦ Seasonal updates
◦ Annual assessment

2. Ongoing Practices:
◦ One-in-one-out rule
◦ Regular cleaning

- Thoughtful additions
- Purposeful sharing
- Continuous evaluation

Sharing Your Success

1. Teaching Others:

- Family guidance
- Friend support
- Community sharing
- Experience offering
- Story telling

2. Building Community:

- Reading groups
- Declutter circles
- Sharing systems
- Support networks
- Learning communities

James, age 87, spreads the joy: "I help other seniors organize their books now. Seeing their relief and happiness when they finish reminds me of my own journey."

Looking Forward

Maintaining Momentum

1. Regular Review:

- Monthly assessments
- Seasonal updates
- Annual planning
- Collection evaluation
- System adjustments

2. Continued Growth:

- New interests
- Fresh perspectives
- Learning opportunities
- Reading adventures
- Social connections

Creating Lasting Change

1. Sustainable Practices:

- Simple systems

- Regular maintenance
- Flexible approaches
- Adaptable solutions
- Ongoing evaluation

2. Future Planning:
- Changing needs
- Family involvement
- Legacy creation
- Collection evolution
- Continuous improvement

Success Stories

Mary, age 92: "A year after decluttering my books, I'm still discovering benefits. I know where everything is, I actually read what I have, and my home feels peaceful."

David, age 88: "My organized library has become a family gathering place. My grandchildren come to choose books, and we have wonderful discussions about what we're reading."

Common Challenges and Solutions

"Missing Old Books"

Solution: Keep photos and notes about special books you've passed along

"Maintaining Organization"

Solution: Use simple, regular routines rather than major efforts

"Resisting New Books"

Solution: Apply the one-in-one-out rule consistently

"Sharing Difficulties"

Solution: Start small and build sharing networks gradually

Chapter Summary

- Curated collections bring freedom
- Space creates opportunities
- Balance serves present needs
- Celebration maintains motivation
- Success builds lasting change

Action Steps

1. This Week:
- Document your progress

- Celebrate achievements
- Share your story
- Plan next steps

2. This Month:

- Review systems
- Adjust routines
- Connect with others
- Set new goals

3. Long Term:

- Maintain balance
- Continue learning
- Build community
- Share wisdom

Final Reflection Questions

As you complete your journey, consider:

1. How has your relationship with books changed?
2. What unexpected benefits have you discovered?
3. What wisdom would you share with others?
4. How will you continue growing and learning?

Remember: A well-curated book collection isn't about having fewer books – it's about having the right books for your life today, arranged in ways that bring you joy and make reading a pleasure rather than a burden.

Your New Chapter

When Martha finished organizing her books, she sat in her reading chair and looked around her newly arranged room. "For the first time in years," she says, "I can find every book I want, and each one brings me joy." Like Martha, you've now learned how to create a book collection that works for your current life while honoring your reading journey.

What We've Learned Together

Throughout this book, we've explored how to make your book collection more manageable and meaningful:

1. Understanding Your Books

• Books aren't just possessions – they're part of your life story

• Different books serve different purposes in your life

• Not every book needs to stay with you forever

• Your needs and interests change over time

2. Creating Safe Spaces

• Proper book storage protects both you and your books

• Accessibility matters more than quantity

• Good organization prevents accidents

• Regular maintenance keeps spaces safe and clean

3. Embracing New Ways of Reading

- Digital options can complement physical books
- Audiobooks and e-readers offer new possibilities
- Technology can make reading easier as we age
- Multiple formats serve different needs

4. Sharing and Connecting

- Books can build bridges between generations
- Thoughtful sharing extends books' impact
- Community connections enrich reading life
- Your books can help others

Moving Forward

As you continue your journey with books, remember these key principles:

Maintaining Your Space

Keep your reading space working well by:

- Regular light cleaning
- Returning books to their places
- Checking for safety issues
- Adjusting as needs change

Eleanor, age 85, shares her routine: "Every evening, I spend five minutes straightening my books and dusting any surfaces I've used. This small habit keeps everything manageable."

Staying Flexible

Your needs will continue to change:

- Be open to new reading formats
- Adjust book storage as needed
- Try different organization methods
- Accept that preferences evolve

Building Connections

Books can continue creating connections:

- Share stories with family
- Join reading communities
- Participate in book discussions
- Pass along reading wisdom

Robert, age 92, found new purpose: "I now read with my great-grandchildren over video chat. The books I kept are helping build bonds across four generations."

Common Questions Answered

As you move forward, you might still have questions. Here are answers to common concerns:

"What if I need a book I gave away?"

• Libraries can often provide copies

• Digital versions may be available

• Consider if you really need the physical book

• Remember why you chose to let it go

"How do I resist collecting more books?"

• Use the one-in-one-out rule

• Consider space limitations

• Focus on current interests

• Try digital alternatives

"What about books I might want later?"

• Trust your initial decisions

• Remember storage constraints

• Consider future accessibility

• Think about practical needs

Creating Lasting Change

To maintain your progress:

1. Regular Review

• Monthly space checks

• Seasonal adjustments

• Annual evaluations

• Collection updates

2. Thoughtful Additions

• Consider space available

• Evaluate real needs

• Think about accessibility

• Plan for storage

3. Continued Sharing

• Update family about available books

• Maintain donation connections

• Share reading experiences

• Offer guidance to others

Looking Ahead

Your reading life can continue to grow and evolve:
• Try new genres and formats
• Connect with other readers
• Share your reading wisdom
• Create reading traditions

Helen, age 88, embraces change: "I now read more than ever, just differently. Some books on my tablet, some audio, and my special books within easy reach. It's perfect for how I live now."

Final Thoughts

Remember:
• A well-organized book collection brings peace
• Reading should bring joy, not stress
• Books can continue building connections
• Your reading life can adapt with you

Sarah, age 90, sums it up well: "My books now tell not just their own stories, but the story of my life. Each one has its place, and together they make my home a place of joy and memories."

Your journey with books isn't ending – it's entering a new chapter. May your reading bring you continued joy, connection, and discovery in the years ahead.